PAPER DESIGNS

Creative Cut-and-Paste Art Projects

Written and Illustrated by Jerome C. Brown

FEARON TEACHER AIDS
Simon & Schuster Supplementary Education Group

Mastery Masters™
Blackline Masters

Cover designer: Joe di Chiarro

Entire contents copyright c 1983 by Fearon Teacher Aids, PO Box 280, Carthage, IL 62321. Permission is hereby granted to reproduce the materials in this book for noncommercial classroom and individual use.

ISBN-0-8224-5193-X

Printed in the United States of America.

1. 9 8 7 6 5

CONTENTS

Introduction

Simple Cut-and-Paste Designs
    Extended Apple Design   1
    Extended Flower Design   2
    Extended Fish Design   3
    All-Over Cutout Design   4
    Cutout Circle Design   5
    Big Butterfly Design   6
    Your Name Design   7
    Your Name Monster   8

Positive and Negative Designs
    Positive and Negative Big Butterfly   9
    Three Positive and Negative Butterflies   10
    Positive and Negative Leaves   11
    Double Positive and Negative Design   12
    Positive and Negative Fold-Out Design   13
    Positive and Negative Fold-Out/Fold-In Design   14
    Positive and Negative Diagonal Design   15
    Positive and Negative Mask Design   16
    Positive and Negative Flames   17
    Positive and Negative Valentine Design   18
    Positive and Negative Diamond Design   19
    Positive and Negative Trees   20
    Positive and Negative Fish   21
    Positive and Negative Christmas Ornaments   22
    Positive and Negative Spring Theme   23
    Checkerboard Positive and Negative Leaves   24
    Positive and Negative Halloween Shapes   25

Cut-and-Paste Compositions
    Cut-and-Paste Mask Design (Vertical)   26
    Cut-and-Paste Mask Design (Horizontal)   27
    Cut-and-Paste Butterfly Design   28
    Cut-and-Paste Leaf Design   29
    Cut-and-Paste Bird   30
    Cut-and-Paste Paper Mosaic   31

Cut-Paper Weaving	32
Fish with Scales	33
Fish Under Water	34
Cut-Paper Abstract	35
Torn-Paper Abstract	36
Cut-and-Paste Magazine Collage	37
Cut-and-Paste Flowers	38
Cut-and-Paste Flower Basket	39
Cut-and-Paste Still Life	40
Cut-and-Paste Seascape	41

INTRODUCTION

Paper Designs contains 41 blackline Mastery Masters™—duplicatable activity sheets featuring original paper-and-paste construction projects. The projects are suitable for children in the elementary grades. Each sheet provides full instructions and diagrams, but younger children will undoubtedly require additional help and demonstration.

Teachers or other supervising adults should select, then photocopy, individual worksheets so that each child has a sheet to work from. These papercraft projects can supplement an art program or be used in a learning center. Encourage children to display or present their finished constructions in the classroom or at home.

In each section of this book, the projects are arranged with the easiest ones first and the more complicated ones last. Feel free to change any design to suit your group's needs. For example, instead of a butterfly, you might use a heart or even a circle.

All the projects in this book can be made with construction paper, which is referred to as art paper. You may also want to try using wallpaper samples, newspaper, colorful magazine ads, or bright scraps of gift wrap. Children can make striking designs with two or three colors—or more!

These projects have been carefully prepared to provide every child who tries them with a successful experience in artistic creativity. However, whenever there is time, children will benefit most if the projects are treated as experiments in design. Particularly in the last section, children will be able to develop individual aesthetics more fully if they have a chance to critique their own work and then do a project again in a different way. Following are suggestions that will help ensure successful results.

Fold-Cutting. The easiest way to achieve symmetry in cutouts is to fold the paper in half and draw half the figure along the fold. Cut out the half with the paper still folded.

Multiple Cutting. Cutting two or more pieces of paper at once is a timesaving technique. Generally, even blunt scissors are able to cut two pieces of paper at a time. However, never try to cut more than the scissors will allow. When cutting flowers, and several are needed, select two, three, or four colors of art paper. Draw a flower design on the top piece and cut out all at once.

Tearing Shapes. Practice tearing paper into squares before you use this method to make designs. You may want to use newspaper or scraps for practice.

Composition. Think about your composition before you paste. Move the pieces around until you like the arrangement. Is there a center of interest? Do the shapes and colors balance each other?

Spot Pasting. Don't use too much paste—spot paste instead. Spot pasting means using tiny drops of paste or glue here and there, rather than smearing paste all over a piece of paper. It will keep paste from getting on the background or lumping up under the design.

Supplies and Equipment. Reliable proven materials and dependable tools make for successful art projects. If you are purchasing your own equipment and supplies, look for reliable brand names and choose carefully.

EXTENDED APPLE DESIGN

MATERIALS

6" X 9" ART PAPER FOR BACKGROUND
4½" X 6" ART PAPER FOR APPLE
SCISSORS AND PASTE
PENCIL AND ERASER

A

B

PROCEDURE

1. DRAW APPLE ON 4½" X 6" ART PAPER WITH PENCIL.
2. DRAW CURVED LINES THROUGH APPLE WITH A PENCIL (FIG. A).
3. CUT APPLE OUT.
4. CUT ON CURVED LINES.
5. LAY EACH SECTION IN PLACE ON 6" X 9" BACKGROUND PAPER. ALLOW ABOUT ¼" BETWEEN SECTIONS.
6. PASTE EACH PIECE IN PLACE.

PAPER DESIGNS REPRODUCIBLE PAGE, © 1983

EXTENDED FLOWER DESIGN

MATERIALS

9" X 12" ART PAPER FOR BACKGROUND
6" X 9" ART PAPER FOR FLOWER
SCISSORS AND PASTE
PENCIL AND ERASER

A

PROCEDURE

1. DRAW FLOWER ON 6" X 9" ART PAPER WITH PENCIL.
2. DRAW LINES THROUGH FLOWER WITH PENCIL (FIG. A).
3. CUT FLOWER OUT.
4. CUT ON LINES.
5. LAY EACH SECTION IN PLACE ON 9" X 12" BACKGROUND PAPER (FIG. B). ALLOW ABOUT 1/4" BETWEEN SECTIONS.
6. PASTE EACH PIECE IN PLACE.

EXTENDED FISH DESIGN

MATERIALS

9" X 12" ART PAPER FOR BACKGROUND
6" X 9" ART PAPER FOR FISH
SCISSORS AND PASTE
PENCIL AND ERASER

PROCEDURE
1. DRAW FISH ON 6" X 9" ART PAPER.
2. DRAW CURVED LINES THROUGH FISH WITH PENCIL.
3. CUT OUT FISH.
4. CUT ON CURVED LINES.
5. LAY EACH SECTION IN PLACE ON 9" X 12" BACKGROUND PAPER. ALLOW ABOUT 1/4" BETWEEN SECTIONS.
6. PASTE EACH PIECE IN PLACE.

PAPER DESIGNS REPRODUCIBLE PAGE, © 1983

ALL-OVER CUTOUT DESIGN

MATERIALS
9" X 12" ART PAPER FOR BACKGROUND
9" X 12" ART PAPER FOR DESIGN
PENCIL AND PAPER
SCISSORS AND PASTE

A

PROCEDURE
1. FOLD PAPER FOR DESIGN INTO FOURTHS.
2. DRAW A DESIGN ON ONE OF THE FOUR SIDES WITH PENCIL (FIG. A).
3. CUT OUT THE DESIGN.
4. PASTE CUTOUT ONTO BACKGROUND SHEET.

PAPER DESIGNS REPRODUCIBLE PAGE, © 1983

CUTOUT CIRCLE DESIGN

MATERIALS
9" X 9" SQUARE OF ART PAPER FOR BACKGROUND
9" X 9" SQUARE OF ART PAPER FOR DESIGN
COMPASS
PENCIL AND ERASER
SCISSORS AND PASTE

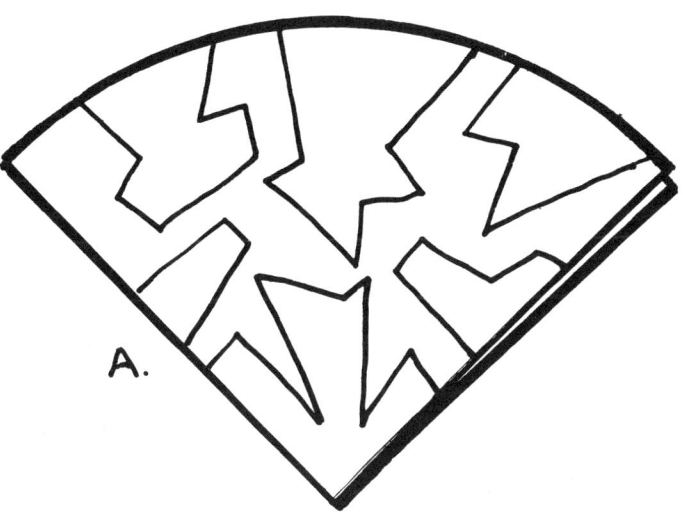

A.

PROCEDURE
1. USE COMPASS TO MAKE CIRCLES OUT OF BOTH 9" SQUARES.
2. CUT OUT CIRCLES.
3. FOLD ONE CIRCLE INTO FOURTHS (FIG A).
4. DRAW A DESIGN ON ONE SIDE.
5. CUT OUT THE DESIGN.
6. PASTE DESIGN ONTO BACKGROUND.

PAPER DESIGNS REPRODUCIBLE PAGE, © 1983

BIG BUTTERFLY DESIGN

MATERIALS

9" x 12" ART PAPER FOR BACKGROUND
9" x 12" ART PAPER FOR DESIGN
3" x 4" ART PAPER FOR DECORATIVE DETAILS
PENCIL AND ERASER
SCISSORS AND PASTE

A

PROCEDURE

1. FOLD PAPER FOR DESIGN IN HALF THE LONG WAY.
2. DRAW BUTTERFLY SHAPE IN PENCIL (FIG. A).
3. CUT BUTTERFLY OUT.
4. FOLD BACKGROUND PAPER IN HALF THE LONG WAY.
5. LINE UP FOLD ON BUTTERFLY WITH FOLD ON BACKGROUND.
6. PASTE BUTTERFLY IN PLACE.
7. CUT DETAILS FOR WING DESIGN OUT OF 3" x 4" PAPER AND PASTE ON.

PAPER DESIGNS REPRODUCIBLE PAGE, © 1983

YOUR NAME DESIGN

MATERIALS
9" x 12" ART PAPER FOR BACKGROUND
9" x 12" ART PAPER FOR DESIGN
PENCIL AND ERASER
SCISSORS AND PASTE

A.

B.

PROCEDURE
1. FOLD PAPER FOR DESIGN IN HALF.
2. WRITE FIRST OR LAST NAME IN LARGE LETTERS ALONG THE FOLDED EDGE (FIG. A).
3. DRAW PARALLEL LINES ON EACH SIDE OF ORIGINAL LINE TO THICKEN IT (FIG. B).
4. CUT OUT DESIGN AND PASTE ONTO BACKGROUND PAPER.

YOUR NAME MONSTER

MATERIALS
9" X 12" ART PAPER FOR BACKGROUND
9" X 12" ART PAPER FOR DESIGN
ART PAPER SCRAPS
PENCIL AND ERASER
SCISSORS AND PASTE

A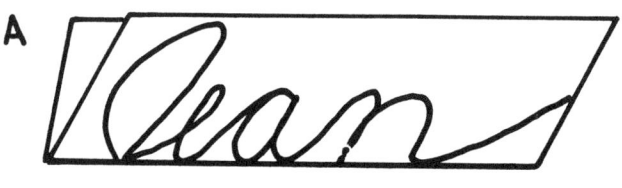

B

PROCEDURE
1. FOLD PAPER FOR DESIGN IN HALF.
2. WRITE NAME IN LARGE LETTERS ALONG FOLD (FIG. A).
3. DRAW PARALLEL LINES AROUND THE ORIGINAL LINE TO THICKEN IT (FIG. B).
4. CUT OUT DESIGN.
5. PASTE DESIGN ONTO BACKGROUND SHEET.
6. USE SCRAP PIECES TO MAKE MONSTER FEATURES. PASTE ONTO DESIGN.

POSITIVE AND NEGATIVE BIG BUTTERFLY

MATERIALS

9" x 12" ART PAPER FOR BACKGROUND
6" x 9" ART PAPER FOR BUTTERFLY
PENCIL AND ERASER
SCISSORS AND PASTE

A

PROCEDURE

1. DRAW HALF A BUTTERFLY ON 6" x 9" SHEET (FIG. A).
2. CAREFULLY CUT OUT DESIGN.
3. ARRANGE BOTH PIECES ON BACKGROUND AS SHOWN.
4. PASTE IN PLACE.

THREE POSITIVE AND NEGATIVE BUTTERFLIES

MATERIALS
9" x 12" ART PAPER FOR BACKGROUND
4½" x 12" ART PAPER FOR BUTTERFLIES
PENCIL AND ERASER
SCISSORS AND PASTE
FELT-TIP PENS

PROCEDURE
1. DIVIDE 4½" x 12" PAPER INTO THIRDS.
2. DRAW HALF A BUTTERFLY ON EACH THIRD (FIG. A).
3. CUT OUT DESIGNS.
4. PASTE BOTH THE BUTTERFLY HALVES AND THE PIECE FROM WHICH THEY WERE CUT ON BACKGROUND AS SHOWN.
5. DRAW ON ANTENNAE.

A

POSITIVE AND NEGATIVE LEAVES

MATERIALS
6" X 12" ART PAPER FOR BACKGROUND
3" X 12" ART PAPER FOR DESIGN
PENCIL AND ERASER
SCISSORS AND PASTE

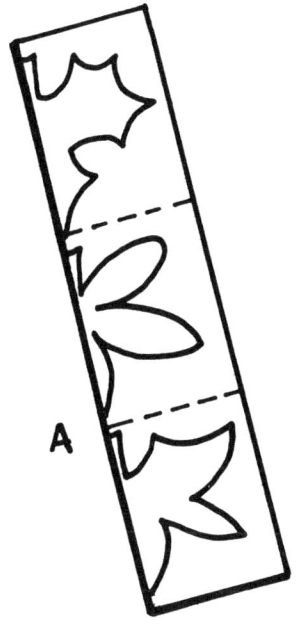
A

PROCEDURE
1. DIVIDE PAPER FOR DESIGN INTO THIRDS.
2. DRAW HALF A LEAF ON EACH THIRD (FIG. A). TRACE SHAPES OF COLLECTED LEAVES OR DRAW YOUR OWN.
3. CUT OUT DESIGNS.
4. PASTE BOTH THE LEAF HALVES AND THE PIECE FROM WHICH THEY WERE CUT ON BACKGROUND AS SHOWN.
5. PASTE IN PLACE.

DOUBLE POSITIVE AND NEGATIVE DESIGN

MATERIALS
9" X 12" ART PAPER FOR BACKGROUND
2 PIECES OF 2½" X 9" ART PAPER FOR DESIGNS
SCISSORS AND PASTE
PENCIL AND ERASER

A

PROCEDURE
1. DIVIDE A 2½" X 9" SHEET INTO THIRDS.
2. DRAW AN ABSTRACT SHAPE IN EACH AREA (FIG. A).
3. PUT BOTH 2½" X 9" SHEETS TOGETHER. CUT DESIGNS OUT OF BOTH PIECES AT THE SAME TIME.
4. ARRANGE BOTH 2½" X 9" STRIPS AND CUTOUTS ON BACKGROUND AS SHOWN.
5. PASTE ALL PIECES IN PLACE.

POSITIVE AND NEGATIVE FOLD-OUT DESIGN

MATERIALS
9" x 12" ART PAPER FOR BACKGROUND
4½" X 6" ART PAPER FOR DESIGN
PENCIL AND ERASER
SCISSORS AND PASTE

A

PROCEDURE
1. CUT 4½" X 6" RECTANGLE INTO AN IRREGULAR SHAPE (FIG. A).
2. DRAW AN ABSTRACT SHAPE ALONG EACH SIDE (FIG. A).
3. CUT OUT SHAPES. ARRANGE ALL PIECES ON BACKGROUND AS SHOWN.
4. PASTE ALL PIECES IN PLACE.

POSITIVE AND NEGATIVE FOLD-OUT/FOLD-IN DESIGN

MATERIALS
9" X 12" ART PAPER FOR BACKGROUND
4½" X 6" ART PAPER FOR DESIGN
PENCIL AND ERASER
SCISSORS AND PASTE

A

PROCEDURE
1. DRAW AN ABSTRACT DESIGN ON EACH SIDE OF THE 4½" X 6" SHEET.
2. WITHIN EACH DESIGN, DRAW ANOTHER SMALLER DESIGN. (FIG. A).
3. CUT OUT ALL THE DESIGNS. BE CAREFUL NOT TO MIX THEM UP.
4. ARRANGE THE PIECES AS SHOWN AND PASTE IN PLACE.

POSITIVE AND NEGATIVE DIAGONAL DESIGN

MATERIALS

9" x 12" ART PAPER FOR BACKGROUND
PRECUT DIAGONAL HALF OF 9"x12"
  ART PAPER
PENCIL AND PAPER
SCISSORS AND PASTE

A

PROCEDURE

1. DRAW DESIGN ON DIAGONAL SHEET.
2. ARRANGE CUT PIECE AND CUTOUT ON BACKGROUND PAPER.
3. PASTE IN PLACE.

PAPER DESIGNS REPRODUCIBLE PAGE, © 1983

POSITIVE AND NEGATIVE MASK DESIGN

MATERIALS
9" X 12" ART PAPER FOR BACKGROUND
4½" X 12" ART PAPER FOR MASK
PENCIL AND ERASER
SCISSORS AND PASTE

A

PROCEDURE
1. DRAW HALF A MASK ON 4½" X 12" SHEET (FIG. A).
2. ARRANGE CUT PIECE AND CUTOUT ON BACKGROUND PAPER.
3. PASTE IN PLACE.

PAPER DESIGNS   REPRODUCIBLE PAGE, © 1983

POSITIVE AND NEGATIVE FLAMES

MATERIALS
12" X 18" ART PAPER FOR BACKGROUND
9" X 12" ART PAPER FOR FLAMES
PENCIL AND ERASER
SCISSORS AND PASTE

PROCEDURE
1. DRAW FLAMES ON 9" X 12" ART PAPER (FIG. A).
2. CUT OUT DESIGN. ARRANGE CUT PIECE AND CUTOUT ON BACKGROUND PAPER.
3. PASTE BOTH PIECES IN PLACE. SPOT PASTE TO AVOID GETTING EXCESS PASTE ON THE BACKGROUND.

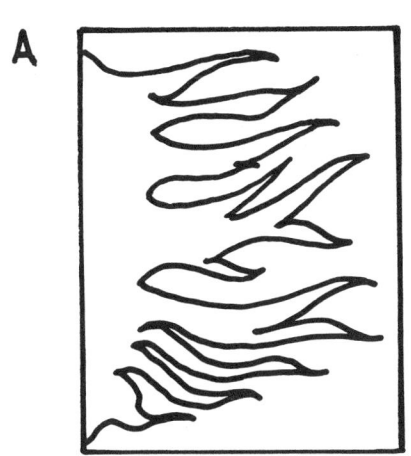

A

POSITIVE AND NEGATIVE VALENTINE DESIGN

MATERIALS

9" X 12" ART PAPER FOR BACKGROUND
4 PIECES OF 3" X 4½" ART PAPER FOR DESIGNS
PENCIL AND ERASER
SCISSORS AND PASTE

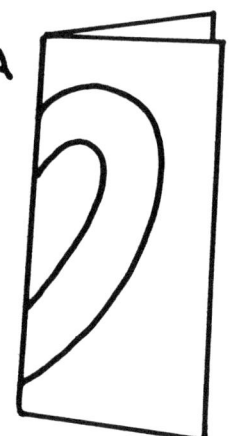
A

PROCEDURE

1. FOLD THE FOUR 3" X 4½" PIECES IN HALF.
2. DRAW HALF-HEARTS IN VARIOUS SIZES ALONG THE FOLDS. DRAW SOME HEARTS WITHIN HEARTS (FIGS. A AND B).
3. CUT OUT HEARTS.
4. PASTE CUT PIECES ON BACKGROUND IN CHECKERBOARD DESIGN AS SHOWN.
5. ARRANGE HEART CUTOUTS IN EACH AREA. PASTE IN PLACE.

B

POSITIVE AND NEGATIVE DIAMOND DESIGN

MATERIALS

9" X 12" ART PAPER FOR BACKGROUND
4 PIECES OF 3" X 4½" ART PAPER FOR DESIGN
PENCIL AND ERASER
SCISSORS AND PASTE

PROCEDURE

1. FOLD THE FOUR 3" X 4½" PIECES IN HALF.
2. DRAW DESIGN ON FOLDED SHEETS (FIG. A).
3. CUT OUT DESIGNS. ARRANGE CUT PIECES AND CUTOUTS ON BACKGROUND.
4. PASTE IN PLACE.

PAPER DESIGNS REPRODUCIBLE PAGE, © 1983

POSITIVE AND NEGATIVE TREES

MATERIALS

9" X 12" ART PAPER FOR BACKGROUND
2 PIECES OF 4½" X 6" ART PAPER FOR DESIGN
PENCIL AND ERASER
SCISSORS AND PASTE

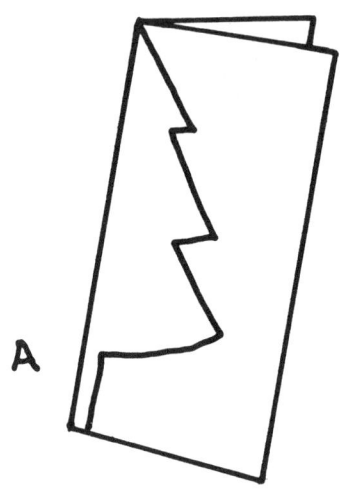

A

PROCEDURE

1. FOLD THE TWO 4½" X 6" SHEETS IN HALF.
2. DRAW HALF A TREE ALONG EACH FOLD (FIG. A).
3. CUT OUT TREE DESIGNS.
4. ARRANGE PIECES ON BACKGROUND SHEET AS SHOWN.
5. PASTE IN PLACE.

POSITIVE AND NEGATIVE FISH

MATERIALS

9" X 12" ART PAPER FOR BACKGROUND
2 PIECES OF 4½" X 6" ART PAPER FOR FISH SHAPES
PENCIL AND ERASER
SCISSORS AND PASTE

PROCEDURE

1. FOLD EACH 4½" X 6" SHEET IN HALF.
2. DRAW HALF A FISH SHAPE ALONG EACH FOLD (FIGS. A AND B).
3. CUT OUT FISH SHAPES.
4. ARRANGE POSITIVE AND NEGATIVE SHAPES ON BACKGROUND PAPER.
5. PASTE IN PLACE.

POSITIVE AND NEGATIVE CHRISTMAS ORNAMENTS

MATERIALS
9" X 12" ART PAPER FOR BACKGROUND
2 PIECES OF 4½" X 6" ART PAPER
  FOR DESIGN
PENCIL AND ERASER
SCISSORS AND PASTE

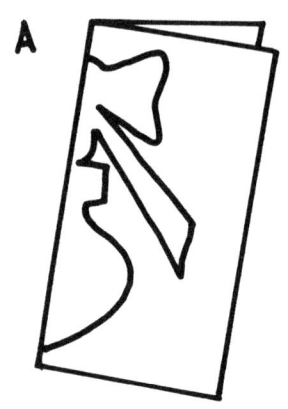
A

PROCEDURE
1. FOLD 4½" X 6" SHEETS IN HALF.
2. DRAW HALF AN ORNAMENT ALONG FOLD ON EACH SHEET (FIGS. A AND B).
3. CUT OUT DESIGNS.
4. ARRANGE CUT PIECES AND CUT-OUTS ON BACKGROUND.
5. PASTE PIECES IN PLACE.

POSITIVE AND NEGATIVE SPRING THEME

MATERIALS

9" X 12" ART PAPER FOR BACKGROUND
2 PIECES OF 4½" X 6" ART PAPER FOR DESIGN
PENCIL AND ERASER
SCISSORS AND PASTE

PROCEDURE

1. FOLD BOTH 4½" X 6" SHEETS IN HALF.
2. DRAW HALF A FLOWER ALONG FOLD OF ONE SHEET (FIG. A).
3. DRAW HALF A RABBIT ALONG FOLD OF OTHER SHEET (FIG. B).
4. CUT OUT DESIGNS.
5. ARRANGE CUT PIECES AND CUT-OUTS ON BACKGROUND.
6. PASTE IN PLACE.

CHECKERBOARD POSITIVE AND NEGATIVE LEAVES

MATERIALS
9" X 12" ART PAPER FOR BACKGROUND
4 PIECES OF 3" X 4½" ART PAPER FOR LEAF DESIGNS
PENCIL AND ERASER
SCISSORS AND PASTE

A

PROCEDURE
1. FOLD THE FOUR 3" X 4½" SHEETS IN HALF (FIG. A).
2. DRAW ONE LEAF DESIGN ALONG FOLDS OF TWO SHEETS (FIG. B).
3. DRAW ANOTHER LEAF DESIGN ALONG FOLDS OF OTHER TWO SHEETS.
4. CUT OUT LEAF DESIGNS. ARRANGE CUT PIECES AND CUTOUTS ON BACKGROUND PAPER.
5. PASTE IN PLACE.

B

POSITIVE AND NEGATIVE HALLOWEEN SHAPES

MATERIALS

9" x 12" ART PAPER FOR BACKGROUND
4 PIECES OF 3" x 4½" ART PAPER FOR DESIGN
PENCIL AND ERASER
SCISSORS AND PASTE
FELT-TIP PEN

PROCEDURE

1. FOLD THE FOUR 3" x 4½" PIECES OF ART PAPER IN HALF (FIG. A).
2. DRAW HALF A PUMPKIN ALONG FOLDS OF TWO SHEETS (FIG. A).
3. DRAW HALF A WITCH DESIGN ALONG FOLDS OF OTHER TWO SHEETS (FIG. B).
4. CUT OUT DESIGNS.
5. ARRANGE CUT PIECES AND CUTOUTS ON BACKGROUND.
6. PASTE IN PLACE. DRAW FACES ON PUMPKINS WITH PEN.

CUT-AND-PASTE MASK DESIGN (VERTICAL)

MATERIALS
9" X 12" ART PAPER FOR BACKGROUND
9" X 12" ART PAPER FOR MASK
ART PAPER SCRAPS
PENCIL AND ERASER
SCISSORS AND PASTE

A

B

PROCEDURE
1. FOLD ONE 9" X 12" SHEET IN HALF LENGTHWISE.
2. DRAW HALF A MASK ALONG FOLD (FIG. A).
3. CUT OUT MASK.
4. FOLD BACKGROUND PAPER IN HALF LENGTHWISE.
5. LINE UP MASK FOLD WITH FOLD ON BACKGROUND SHEET AND PASTE IN PLACE.
6. FOLD-CUT FEATURES (GLASSES, EARRINGS, MUSTACHE, EYEBROWS, ETC. SEE FIG. B) OUT OF ART PAPER SCRAPS.
7. ARRANGE DETAILS ON MASK. PASTE IN PLACE.

PAPER DESIGNS REPRODUCIBLE PAGE, © 1983

CUT-AND-PASTE MASK DESIGN (HORIZONTAL)

MATERIALS

9" x 12" ART PAPER FOR BACKGROUND
9" x 12" ART PAPER FOR MASK
ART PAPER SCRAPS
PENCIL AND ERASER
SCISSORS AND PASTE

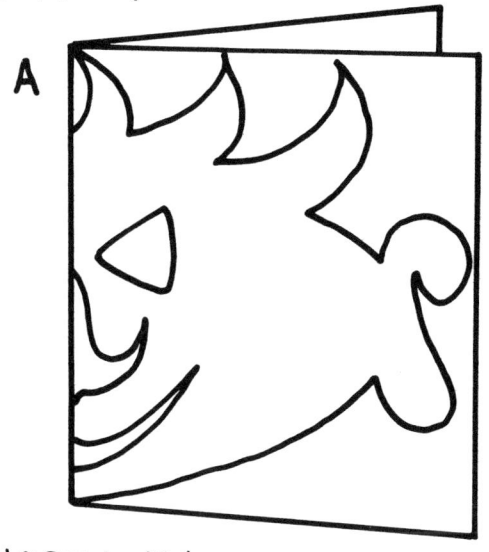
A

PROCEDURE

1. FOLD BOTH 9" x 12" SHEETS THE SHORT WAY.
2. DRAW HALF THE MASK ALONG THE FOLD OF ONE SHEET.
3. CUT OUT MASK (FIG. A).
4. LINE UP FOLD ON MASK WITH FOLD ON BACKGROUND SHEET. PASTE MASK IN PLACE.
5. FOLD-CUT DETAILS USING SCRAPS (GLASSES, HEADDRESS, MOUTH, ETC.).
6. ARRANGE DECORATIONS ON MASK. PASTE IN PLACE.

CUT-AND-PASTE BUTTERFLY DESIGN

MATERIALS

9" X 12" ART PAPER FOR BACKGROUND
2 PIECES OF 6" X 9" ART PAPER FOR BUTTERFLIES
PENCIL AND ERASER
SCISSORS AND PASTE
FELT-TIP PEN

PROCEDURE

1. CUT THE TWO 6" X 9" SHEETS INTO PIECES OF VARIOUS SIZES (FIGS. A, B, AND C).
2. FOLD EACH PIECE IN HALF.
3. DRAW HALF A BUTTERFLY ON EACH PIECE. CUT OUT BUTTERFLIES. ARRANGE ON 9" X 12" SHEET.
4. PASTE CUTOUTS IN PLACE.
5. ADD ANTENNAE TO BUTTERFLIES WITH FELT-TIP PEN.

CUT-AND-PASTE LEAF DESIGN

MATERIALS
9" x 12" ART PAPER FOR BACKGROUND
3 PIECES OF 6" x 9" ART PAPER FOR LEAVES
PENCIL AND ERASER
SCISSORS AND PASTE

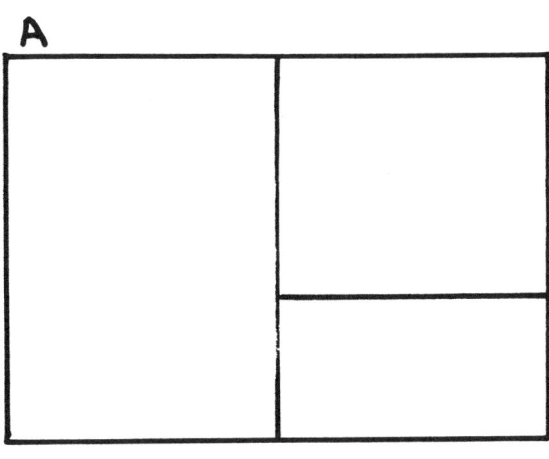

PROCEDURE
1. CUT 6" x 9" SHEETS AS SHOWN IN FIG. A TO ENSURE THREE DIFFERENT-SIZED LEAVES.
2. FOLD EACH PIECE IN HALF. DRAW LEAF SHAPES ON FOLDED PAPER (FIG. B).
3. CUT OUT LEAVES.
4. ARRANGE OVERLAPPING LEAVES ON BACKGROUND PAPER.
5. PASTE IN PLACE.

CUT-AND-PASTE BIRD

MATERIALS

9" X 12" ART PAPER FOR BACKGROUND
6" X 9" ART PAPER FOR TREE
2 PIECES OF 4½" X 6" ART PAPER FOR BIRD
ART PAPER SCRAPS
PENCIL AND ERASER
SCISSORS AND PASTE

A

B

PROCEDURE

1. DRAW AND CUT OUT TREE BRANCH.
2. DRAW AND CUT OUT LEAVES.
3. ARRANGE BRANCH AND LEAVES ON BACKGROUND SHEET. PASTE IN PLACE.
4. DRAW BIRD'S BODY AND BEAK ON ONE 4½" X 6" SHEET (FIG. A).
5. DRAW HEAD AND FEATHERS ON SECOND 4½" X 6" SHEET (FIG. B). CUT OUT.
6. USE SCRAPS FOR EYE AND WING.
7. ARRANGE PIECES ON BACKGROUND SHEET.
8. PASTE IN PLACE.

PAPER DESIGNS REPRODUCIBLE PAGE, © 1983

CUT-AND-PASTE PAPER MOSAIC

MATERIALS

9" X 12" ART PAPER FOR BACKGROUND
4 PIECES OF 4½" X 6" ART PAPER FOR DESIGN
PENCIL AND ERASER
SCISSORS AND PASTE

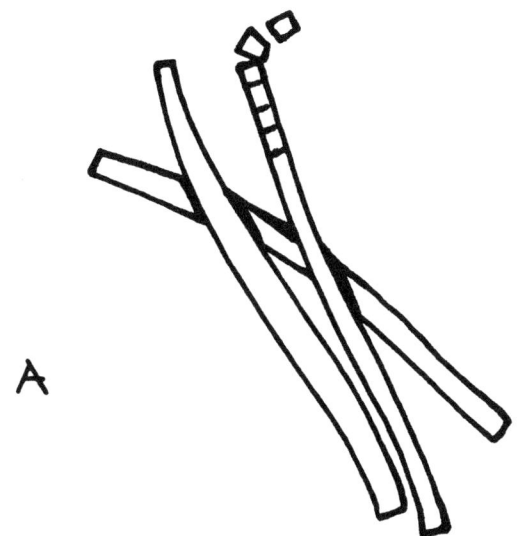

A

B

PROCEDURE

1. DRAW FLOWER IN VASE OR ANOTHER DESIGN ON BACKGROUND SHEET.
2. CUT 4½" X 6" SHEETS INTO STRIPS ½" WIDE (FIG. A).
3. CUT THE STRIPS INTO ½" SQUARES (FIG. B).
4. ARRANGE SQUARES ON ONE PART OF DESIGN AT A TIME. SHAPE AS NECESSARY. PASTE IN PLACE.
5. FILL IN SPACE AROUND DESIGN SO 9" X 12" IS COVERED WITH A MOSAIC OF CUT PAPER.

PAPER DESIGNS REPRODUCIBLE PAGE, © 1983

CUT-PAPER WEAVING

MATERIALS

9" X 12" ART PAPER FOR BACKGROUND
2 PIECES OF 5" X 9" ART PAPER FOR WEAVING
PENCIL AND ERASER
SCISSORS AND PASTE

A

B

C

PROCEDURE

1. FOLD 9" X 12" SHEET IN HALF.
2. FOLD DOWN 1-INCH MARGIN ON EACH OPEN END (FIG. A).
3. MAKE EIGHT CUTS (STRAIGHT OR IRREGULAR) FROM CENTER FOLD TO FOLDED MARGINS (FIG. B).
4. UNFOLD BACKGROUND SHEET.
5. CUT EACH 5" X 9" PIECE INTO 1" X 9" STRIPS.
6. WEAVE STRIPS INTO BACKGROUND SHEET (FIG. C).
7. PASTE STRIPS AT EACH END SO THEY WILL NOT SLIP.

PAPER DESIGNS REPRODUCIBLE PAGE, © 1983

FISH WITH SCALES

MATERIALS

9" X 12" ART PAPER FOR BACKGROUND
9" X 12" ART PAPER FOR FISH SHAPE
6" X 9" ART PAPER FOR FISH SCALES
PENCIL AND ERASER
SCISSORS AND PASTE
HOLE PUNCH

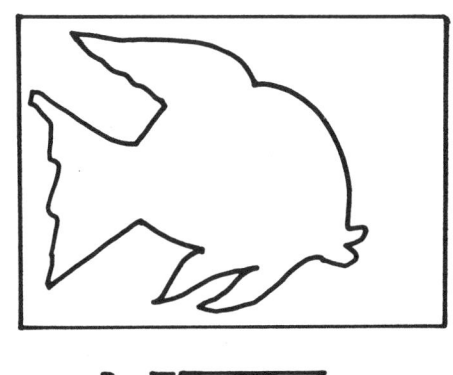

PROCEDURE

1. DRAW FISH SHAPE ON ONE 9"x12" SHEET. CUT OUT SHAPE (FIG. A).
2. PASTE FISH SHAPE ON BACKGROUND.
3. CUT OUT AS MANY SCALES AS NEEDED (FIG. B).
4. PASTE OVERLAPPING SCALES ONTO FISH. START AT TAIL AND WORK TOWARD HEAD (FIG. C).
5. USE SCRAP PIECES TO MAKE EYE.
6. USE HOLE PUNCH TO CREATE BUBBLES. PASTE BUBBLES IN PLACE.

FISH UNDER WATER

MATERIALS
3 PIECES OF 9"x12" ART PAPER
PENCIL AND ERASER
SCISSORS AND PASTE

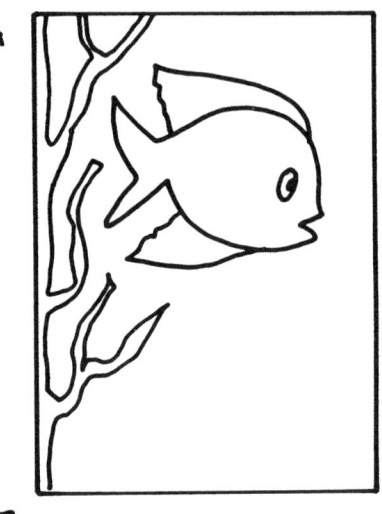
A

B

C

PROCEDURE
1. USE ONE 9"x12" SHEET FOR BACKGROUND
2. ON THE OTHER TWO PIECES, DRAW FISH AND UNDERWATER PLANTS (FIGS. A AND B).
3. CUT OUT FISH, PLANTS, AND BUBBLES. ARRANGE ON BACKGROUND.
4. PASTE PIECES IN PLACE (FIG. C).
5. MAKE EYES OUT OF SCRAPS AND PASTE ON.

CUT-PAPER ABSTRACT

MATERIALS
9" x 12" ART PAPER FOR BACKGROUND
4 PIECES OF 6" x 9" ART PAPER FOR DESIGN
PENCIL AND ERASER
SCISSORS AND PASTE

PROCEDURE
1. CUT THE PIECES OF 6" x 9" PAPER INTO MANY SHAPES. MAKE SMALL, MEDIUM, AND LARGE SIZES. TRY USING PATTERNED PAPER OR WALLPAPER TOO.
2. THINK ABOUT THE DESIGN YOU WANT TO CREATE.
   - TRY TO BALANCE SHAPES AND COLORS.
   - MAKE A CENTER OF ATTRACTION.
3. ARRANGE SHAPES ON BACKGROUND.
4. WHEN YOU LIKE THE DESIGN, PASTE THE PIECES IN PLACE.

TORN-PAPER ABSTRACT

MATERIALS
9" x 12" ART PAPER FOR BACKGROUND
3 PIECES OF 4½" x 6" ART PAPER FOR DESIGN
PENCIL AND ERASER
SCISSORS AND PASTE

PROCEDURE
1. THINK ABOUT THE DESIGN YOU WANT TO CREATE. PLAN TO:
   - USE LARGE, MEDIUM, AND SMALL PIECES
   - HAVE THE PIECES OVERLAP
   - HAVE A CENTER OF ATTRACTION
2. TEAR PIECES OF VARYING SIZES AND SHAPES.
3. ARRANGE THEM ON BACKGROUND SHEET.
4. PASTE SHAPES INTO FINAL POSITION.

CUT-AND-PASTE MAGAZINE COLLAGE

MATERIALS

9" x 12" ART PAPER FOR BACKGROUND
3 PIECES OF 6" x 9" ART PAPER FOR DESIGN
MAGAZINES, COMICS, OR NEWSPAPERS
PENCIL AND ERASER
SCISSORS AND PASTE

PROCEDURE

1. CUT THE THREE PIECES OF 6" x 9" PAPER INTO A VARIETY OF SHAPES AND SIZES.
2. CUT OUT PICTURES AND WORDS FROM MAGAZINES, COMICS, OR NEWSPAPERS. CHOOSE A SINGLE THEME, IF YOU LIKE.
3. ARRANGE THE CUT SHAPES AND CUT-OUTS ON THE BACKGROUND PAPER.
4. WHEN YOU LIKE THE DESIGN, PASTE PIECES IN PLACE.

CUT-AND-PASTE FLOWERS

MATERIALS

9" x 12" ART PAPER FOR BACKGROUND
4 PIECES OF 6" x 9" ART PAPER FOR FLOWERS, VASE, AND LEAVES
2" x 9" ART PAPER FOR TABLE
PENCIL AND ERASER
SCISSORS AND PASTE
FELT-TIP PEN

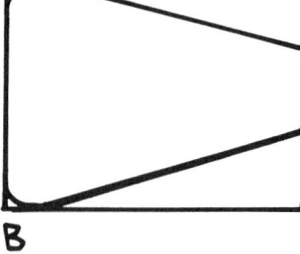

A

B

PROCEDURE

1. DRAW AND CUT OUT THREE 4" x 4" FLOWERS (FIG. A).
2. DRAW AND CUT OUT 4½" x 6" VASE (FIG. B).
3. CUT OUT THREE 1½" x 4½" LEAVES.
4. USE FELT-TIP PEN TO DRAW LEAF VEINS.
5. PASTE PAPER FOR TABLE ON BOTTOM OF BACKGROUND SHEET.
6. ARRANGE PIECES ON BACKGROUND.
7. PASTE IN PLACE.

PAPER DESIGNS REPRODUCIBLE PAGE, © 1983

CUT-AND-PASTE FLOWER BASKET

MATERIALS

9" x 12" ART PAPER FOR BACKGROUND
2 PIECES OF 9" X 12" ART PAPER FOR FLOWERS, FOREGROUND, AND BASKET
4" x 9" ART PAPER FOR TABLE
PENCIL AND ERASER
SCISSORS AND PASTE
FELT-TIP PEN

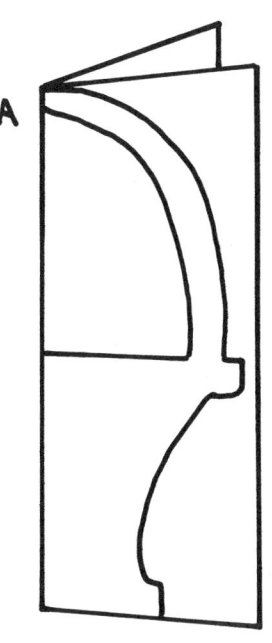

A

PROCEDURE

1. FOLD ONE 9" x 12" SHEET LENGTHWISE. DRAW AND CUT OUT BASKET (FIG. A).
2. ON ANOTHER 9" x 12" SHEET, DRAW AND CUT OUT FOUR 3" x 3" FLOWERS AND ONE 4" x 9" TABLE TOP.
3. PASTE PAPER FOR TABLE ON BOTTOM OF BACKGROUND SHEET.
4. USE SCRAPS FROM BACKGROUND TO MAKE LEAVES. USE FELT-TIP PEN TO DRAW LEAF VEINS.
5. CUT FLOWER CENTERS OUT OF BASKET SCRAPS.
6. ARRANGE CUTOUTS ON BACKGROUND SHEET.
7. PASTE IN PLACE. OUTLINE LEAVES WITH FELT-TIP PEN.

CUT-AND-PASTE STILL LIFE

MATERIALS

9" x 12" ART PAPER FOR BACKGROUND
2 PIECES OF 9" x 12" PAPER FOR
  STILL-LIFE OBJECTS
PENCIL AND ERASER
SCISSORS AND PASTE

PROCEDURE

1. USE BACKGROUND SHEET IN HORIZONTAL POSITION.
2. TEAR PAPER FOR DRAPERY. PASTE ON RIGHT, LEFT, AND ACROSS BOTTOM.
3. DRAW AND CUT OUT BOTTLE AND VASE.
4. DRAW AND CUT OUT FRUIT, FLOWERS, AND LEAVES.
5. ARRANGE PIECES ON BACKGROUND SHEET.
6. PASTE IN PLACE.

CUT-AND-PASTE SEASCAPE

MATERIALS

9" x 12" ART PAPER FOR BACKGROUND
3" x 12" ART PAPER FOR OCEAN
6" x 9" ART PAPER FOR BOAT
ART PAPER SCRAPS
PENCIL AND ERASER
SCISSORS AND PASTE

A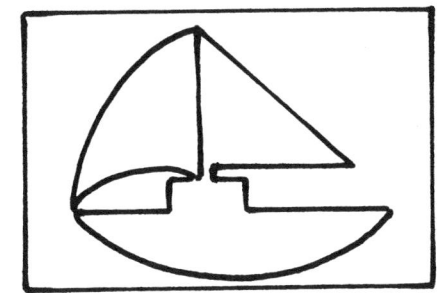

PROCEDURE

1. USE BACKGROUND SHEET HORIZONTALLY.
2. CUT 3" x 12" SHEET FOR OCEAN.
3. DRAW SAILBOAT ON 6" x 9" SHEET AND CUT OUT (FIG. A).
4. TEAR SCRAPS FOR CLOUDS.
5. CUT OUT SEAGULLS.
6. ARRANGE PIECES ON BACKGROUND.
7. PASTE PIECES IN PLACE.

About the Author

Jerome C. Brown is the author of three popular Fearon Teacher Aids, *Cartoon Bulletin Boards, Classroom Cartoons for All Occasions,* and *Christmas in the Classroom.* A retired art teacher, he currently teaches extension classes for teachers.